Becoming Born Again

From Sorority Girl to Saved

Memoir
&
21-Day Devotional

Liz Matory

ISBN: 978-0-578-66477-4

**LIBERTY
LIVES MEDIA**

DEDICATION

I dedicate this book to every soul who wonders, but does not know yet, the power of Jesus Christ. The mere fact that you have kept your heart and mind open is extremely powerful. This world has not made it easy to remain open to God, but knowing that you still will consider your Savior while living in perhaps the most sinful time in history, that is true courage.

Sometimes it can be difficult for us "intellectuals" to accept the truth, but once the Holy Spirit moves within and around you, stay the course.

I am not perfect and I am a sinner, but I am 1000% grateful that I accepted my gift.

God never gives up on us.

We should never give up on Him.

CONTENTS

Psalm 121

I will lift up mine eyes unto the hills, from whence cometh my help.

My help cometh from the LORD, which made heaven and earth.

He will not suffer thy foot to be moved: he that keepeth thee will not slumber.

Behold, he that keepeth Israel shall neither slumber nor sleep.

The LORD is thy keeper: the LORD is thy shade upon thy right hand.

The sun shall not smite thee by day, nor the moon by night.

The LORD shall preserve thee from all evil: he shall preserve thy soul.

The LORD shall preserve thy going out and thy coming in from this time forth, and even for evermore.

BY WAY OF INTRODUCTION.

If you had told me that I'd be a Born Again,
Evangelical Christian sixteen months ago, I
wouldn't have believed you. Just like when I left
the Democrat Party in 2015, I had no idea that I
would leave, become an independent (unaffiliated
they are called in Maryland), then a republican
and now a conservative politician. And yes I'm a
Trump supporter, so indeed that is quite a lot of
change in less than a decade. But because of the
last five years of my life, and this world now to be
honest, I have to share my story to more people
just in case there is someone else like me out
there. Just like when I went through my political
transition, there were no real resources. I felt like

1

I was the only one who wanted to break free.

I left before the #WalkAway Movement or Blexit or Jexit or Lexit or Wexit. And my transition happened while I had already entered into partisan (now hyper-partisan) politics. So many people are leaving the political stronghold of the Democrat Party, but are we getting ourselves prepared for the spiritual war that is raging all around us? In many respects, parties don't matter anymore. I don't know if they really mattered in the first place. So many people can't be bothered. Even more have flat out given up. And the lot of us cannot stand the divisiveness, and do not even know that all of the confusion is purposefully, craftily designed to get us out of our own political system and to suppress us.

I thought that the solution was to become a republican, but I fear that the party is weaker than I would have ever imagined, and that's separate and apart from our duly elected President Donald J. Trump. Don't get me wrong. I would never become a democrat again for reasons that will come clear forthwith. I am extremely proud to have been nominated to Congress by Maryland Republicans in 2018, and I still think it's worth staying in the race for the seat left vacant by the death of Elijah Cummings. But what we are up against, if we are not firm in our dedication to God, anything that anyone will attempt to do from this point onward, will be futile without Christ. It seems like the more conservative I've become, I have noticed that the GOP just try to be the "nice guys/gals" because they think that's what we need. They are unwilling to fight for our true values, and perhaps because they are too difficult or perhaps enough of them don't really share our conservative values in the first place. I know enough of them now to know that redemption is still possible for anyone who will ask for it. I pray that the Holy Spirit moves them to realize that what they are so eager to compromise with is the exact Enemy that we are called to rebuke. Or do they just care about being accepted in their social circles. Only God knows.

This book, *Becoming Born Again*, has been fighting to be written ever since I got saved November 30, 2018. When the Holy Spirit moved inside me, I wanted to trumpet everything that was happening to me to the world. And in some respects I did just that through social media. What I found is that fellow Christians knew exactly what I was talking about, but quite a good number of people still have no clue. I get it. They thought (and still think) that I've jumped off the deep end. Some haters even think it's a gimmick to get elected. Newsflash: the one way not to be accepted by the masses is to become a Christian, just ask Jesus.

Another mental obstacle was whether to talk about politics or not. Politics and religion are supposed to be taboo topics of conversation. But as time went on, it was evident that I could not avoid talking about politics since our culture has been overrun by the ultimate, extremist form of counterculture. We don't talk about any of these topics in polite conversation. Arguably, there is no such thing as polite conversation anymore anyway, so we are all left with two options: remain quiet or Speak Up and Out!

Most people have tapped out and could care less, about politics, about God, about anything really. They just want to be left alone. Given up or exhausted by the divisiveness or hypocrisy or what have you. And believe me, I have thought many times to leave politics all together and question to this day why God shoved me back into such a carnal environment. But just when I feel like throwing in the towel, I am quickly reminded that if I can help one more person see The Truth, it's not only one more soul saved, but also one more prayer warrior in the fight for our lives. We have gotten to a breaking point. A real state of emergency and if we do not identify the obstacles we will never really overcome like the song says.

MY BURDEN.

When you get saved, you get to hear terminology that you have never heard before. Perhaps, you have, but on this side of things, you finally realize the deeper meaning of phrases like *burden* for example. Maybe you have heard, God's laid a burden on my heart for poor kids in Appalachia or something. What that means is that God has moved that person to care so deeply about that someone or something that they feel *called* (or told by God) to be of service to that purpose. Another word for purpose is *mission*.

Perhaps I have been on my mission since the beginning, but everything has become so clear that I can no longer ignore God's calling in my life. I know this is a lot all right off the bat, but since so much is at stake and time is of the essence, I figured to be clear upfront about what we're dealing with, what's at stake, and how to get out of it. Every waking moment from then to now, I know God brought me through for this reason. I just know it. Through every stumble, pain, and heartbreak, I know God can use me to help others out of the darkness. When people hear me proclaiming the Gospel and glorifying God, and they don't know what I'm talking about, most think that I'm being some sort of way. Like "who does she think she is" (Honestly, I have thought that about Christians before became one). Even when I was born again, I looked all around me and thought, "these people are so good, I'm never going to be as good as them."

Many a times when I would share my concerns with fellow Christians, they would acknowledge that the reason why they are how they are is because of what God brought them through. Selfishly, I wanted to know. Like I wanted to see the before and after pictures in a weight loss challenge or something.

But this journey into your new life from

your old is so intense, I know why people didn't want to share. And I've thought about not saying anything more about my past. "The past is your past, leave it there." Having been in the world as intensely as I was knowing how much turbulence that is especially for women and youth, we need to break through with more intension and intensity. So more and more people have the courage to break the chains.

I have chosen to go on the record to document the path from there to here because I know that most of us are still where I was. We have all been taught to live, believe, act, think, question, reject in the exact same manner for the exact same reasons. And if one less person cannot experience what I have, then all of this will be worth it. If there is one other person out there who has experienced what I have, and needs another message to finally heal, then again, all of this was worth it.

MY ROCK BOTTOM.

First things first. Trust your gut. There is a reason why you have a sixth sense, it's really the Holy Spirit, but whatever you want to call it, whenever you feel something is off deep down in your spirit. Trust it. Listen to it. And if it tells you to run, then run.

It may go something like this. You receive an email from an associate, not really a close friend but someone you know from your, let's say, political activities. You check to see what it says since, again, you were not expecting to receive a message from this person, and from the moment you read it, you feel sick. I mean sick sick. Like someone just knocked the wind out of you, sick. You don't know if you're breathing still and all you did was read the words on the screen in front of you.

Something like:

> *"So I don't know how to tell you this, but I was reading through the minutes of a meeting and saw that _____ was in attendance with his wife. I don't know if you know that _____ is married, but I just wanted you to know."*

Panic. Panic. Confusion. Confusion. Cell phone dropped. WTF. (Again, this before I got saved). See, I had been dating _____ for month or so before that email. We had gone on a few dates and talked every day and texted throughout, day and night. He had said that he was divorced. At least I think that's what he said, but in no way shape or form did he say he was still married.

After I called the emailer, I decided to call him. All throughout the conversation that feeling that rapid paced panic had taken over me – I should have cut and run right then and there, but I did not. I chose to believe him. I wanted to believe that he was separated from his wife and that they had an agreement that he would live in the basement and help with the kids before they were old enough. (Yeah, I actually believed that.)

He said that ever since he got back from Iraq, things were never the same from the war. That he had PTSD and was getting treatment from when he was a Marine. (My brother is a Marine, so it made enough sense to me). I admit. I wanted to believe him so badly. I wanted be in a relationship. I thought I had to be. I was 37. Staring 40 in the face. For the past decade, I had one long bad relationship. Another love ODed on me the previous summer and another didn't want to get married again or have children. I admit. I acted out of desperation. I thought I had no other option.

Even when this was all happening I knew he was playing on my vulnerabilities. I knew that I had cried every morning and every night for six months straight after Christopher Barry overdosed on PCP and synthetic weed early in the morning of August 14th 2016. We had never officially dated, but he was the first man to refer to me as his wife. I knew if I did not feel so left behind, I would never have fallen for _____ or accepted any of it. But I really thought I had no choice. He was alive, and he knew what to say to keep me hooked.

For an entire year.

My mom just died and I have to go up to Upstate New York for the funeral because she's a practicing Jew.

My sister was adopted by my father who killed her father when he was a beat cop in Baltimore.

I'm still traumatized when I had to kill a man in Iraq.

And when, again, my gut told me to break up with him for good this time…

It's my mom's one year death anniversary, and when I went up to be with my brother. I got drunk and passed out. I got ill. That's why my ex-girlfriend messaged you (fake Facebook account and who's now a nun can't make this stuff up this really happened) *found me before I died and it's a miracle I survived. No you don't have to come and see me. My brother's driving me back. They let me out of the hospital. They*

took my service weapon away
from me.

None of this was real. Not him getting sick. His mother was alive and well and still a practicing Catholic. His sister wasn't adopted. I don't think he really had a brother. He was never a Marine. He never worked for Homeland Security so he never had a service firearm. His father was never a police officer in Baltimore (actually that may have been the one thing that was true). Mom knit him a navy, red, and gold Marine scarf for Christmas. He sent her flowers. He met half my family. Did I mention he was never a Marine.

All lies. All of it to keep me trapped.

I wouldn't have known any of all this unless I received the text message from his wife. His actually married and lives with shares the same bed still wife, wife. He had left his cell phone at home and I texted him in the morning like we normally did. This time she replied back.

I told you to leave my husband alone.

That's your problem. You need to work that out with him.
I don't know what you're talking about.

Remember, for an entire year, he had sworn they were separated.

She and I exchanged texts back and forth for entire hour. Then she finally invited me to their home so I can finally see the living arrangements for real. Only when I saw with my own eyes did I understand the truth. That was when she told me that they weren't separated at all. That she couldn't wait until she told his mom that he killed her off. I was the fourth woman he's cheated with. Oh and he has the porn problem not their son.

All this revelation was right before Early Voting in 2018. The even sadder thing was half of the Republican Party politicos knew he was married, and only one (1) told me the truth. The ones who knew thought I was ok with being with a married man. I wasn't. The other half was told the same lies as I was.

He would text me "I want to have children with you." And right after, he would text his wife "let's have another baby." Even when we confronted him, he acted like nothing was wrong. He was able to live two separate lives for several years. That was until I fought to get a protective order on him.

He just wouldn't leave me alone.

I've never had to file a protective order before until he tried to kill himself the first time I was aware of it at least. I had just left a community event on Opioid Addiction of all subjects, and he called me. Over and over again. I picked up the phone. I didn't want to, but he kept on calling and calling me. When he got me on the phone we was talking really dark. It reminded me a lot of Christopher months earlier. I hadn't turned back to check on Chris when I heard desperation in his voice the night before he ODed, and his death and the hours preceding will forever be frozen raw in my mind and heart. I had already made it down to Montgomery County, but I turned back to drive back up to Baltimore and drove to ___ house.

His wife was out of town and I really didn't want it to be an issue, but when he showed me the bag of pills that he had been stocking up to kill himself that night, I had to intervene. His son was home and I think his daughter was as well. But she sleeping. His son called his mother and she proceeded to yell at me. I told her what was going on and she called his father. His father lived in Towson (so ___ said). He seemed to have arrived in record time. I will never forget him driving up onto the curb in front of the house. He began to push and shove ____. And he even pushed me off the porch. Even though I just stopped his son from killing himself that night. This was of course after___ had told me that his brother used to molest him when he was younger and that's why he's so messed up. All I could think of was what happened if I hadn't come back. It would have probably been his daughter that would have found him dead in the morning. The same girl who he said I'd be a wonderful stepmom to. So brutal. And yes. There were suicide notes written out.

Before that night, I had never witnessed someone be placed in handcuffs. Before that weekend I had never been in a psych ward before. I never had seen paper pajamas with paper drawstrings before then either. All of it felt like an alternate universe.

Mind you, I never thought I would have found myself in such a relationship. I just couldn't believe it. I couldn't believe any of it. But it happened, just when I had secured the republican nomination for congress at the exact same time as all of this was going on. All the while going back and forth to court to secure a protective order. He even violated the no contact order Primary Night when he called me from someone else's phone.

Baby, we did it.

You know you wouldn't have won this without me.

No one is going to support you in the Party if you don't have me.

Don't hang up. Please don't hang up.

I need you.

I've never been alone.

Who do you think is going to believe you? They have been my friends for years. Why would they believe you over me.

You wouldn't have won this primary if it weren't for me.

Elizabeth. I love you.

Don't report this to the police. Please, I beg you.

Everything seemed to get worse after that. He would show up at parades and walk up to me when he knew I had a stay away order on him. I spent July 4th night at the Dundalk police precinct to file the violation.

Every time I saw my phone ring, I froze. I couldn't plan events throughout the summer because I feared he would show up. His family members began to harass me too on social media. To this day, they still post horrific lies about me on line. As he did in order to retaliate.

I had no idea that he was a classic narcissist and that what I did was the worst thing to do when dealing with one. I had no idea. I was so unaware. I cut off his supply and I found out that he was a part of a den of narcissist that were found out and that hive probably extended out into his friend group in the political party. Something that I would find out a year and a half later.

How could I have fallen for this guy? I felt like such an idiot.

He even was able to stand up in court and describe the nonexistent engagement ring that he told the court he gave me. News to me. Full-on pathological liar. Like oh my word.

And when I couldn't think it would get any worse. It did.

I would receive periodic calls from domestic violence services and the Baltimore County police throughout those months. They would check on me and see how I was doing. (So grateful). And this one time the conversation was a little different.

Ms. Matory are you ok? And are you in a safe place? (As I walked out of the Christmas party that was attending).

Yes, I'm ok.

Well, we're just checking on you and need to inform you that your ex tried to purchase a firearm and was stopped from doing so because of your protective order. There had been two other women who tried to file protective orders on him, but couldn't because their relationships weren't long enough. Yours was the only one that was successful. Please watch your surroundings and call 911 if anything happens.

Ok. Thank you for letting me know. I'm so grateful the other women didn't get hurt.

The weekend went by. My phone went off once or twice and I knew it was him. But I didn't, couldn't answer it. Then the next morning I saw that he had sent me a picture of my nephew's college. I had visited my nephew when I drove up to Upstate when ____ said his mother died. Yes I was that person. I received a text message from a mutual friend before I got "the call" from the police.

Ms. Matory. Have you heard anything about your ex?

I did just now, but I don't know if it's true.

Unfortunately, yes. It is true. He succumbed to self-inflicted asphyxiation, and was found dead in his car in Hunt Valley this morning. He apparently had purchased a hibachi grille and turned on the gas and drank himself to sleep. We just wanted to inform you.

Thank you and thank you for all you have done for us women.

So the morning of Christmas Eve that's how it happened. Just so that everyone from his family to me would always have to remember him. It was always about him.

All I felt was numbness. I knew the wife and everyone would act like nothing happened. But all of it did. And I knew that one of us would not survive 2018. I just knew it. So when it happened, of course it was sad, but it could have been me. *If I can't have you, no one can.* If someone is willing to take their own life, they could probably take mine. That was his fifth or sixth attempt at trying to take his own life over the course of those several months.

So when I tell you, only by the Grace of God am I still alive. I mean it. Right around the time of Early Voting in 2018, just a couple of days after he began to stalk me and I filed my first temporary order at the Towson Courthouse. I still had to continue to campaign. I didn't want to be outside or talk to anyone. All I wanted to do was lay under my covers and hide.

Victory Villa Community Center is where Tina handed me a gospel track. I had never really paid much attention to church invites before, but that time I showed up to church that Sunday morning. I grew up Catholic so the Baptist church service was really different for me. What do you mean three times a week you go to church? Like every

21

time? It's not just three separate masses? Didn't know they weren't called mass. I knew there were no priests, but there was a whole lot of Bible. I had never really read The Bible for real before. I just accepted the readings from mass as sufficient. I had one of course and of course it wasn't KJV, King James Version. I had to learn the significance of that too of course, but there I was going to church church. Only once on Sundays at first and more and more after the months went on.

Even as late as November 30, 2018, I had heard the invitation every time I was in church, but I never really understood what it all was. I didn't know I could stop being a Catholic and that it would be ok. That I could have a personal relationship to Jesus Christ. I had never really heard and read that Jesus was the only way to God, no need to pray to Mary or any of the saints, I could go straight to Jesus Christ myself all the time no priests. He was God on earth, not the pope.

All of these excuses just disappeared when my pastor took the time and personally walked me through the steps.

You can accept the gift. It's available for you.

You just have to receive it and it's yours.

Up until that very moment, I didn't know that it could and would be for me. Maybe other people, but not me. On November 30, 2018, I died and was born again. And if that hadn't happened, _____ death would have simply ruined the rest of what was left of me anyway. Perhaps that's why it made sense to me finally. After all of what had happened I felt like I didn't exist anymore, but if Jesus could use this broken vessel, then I am His.

My greatest prayer is that no one has to hit their rock bottom to get so broken to then only receive Christ. I pray that you choose Christ now. And find yourself a real Bible centered church to help cover you and shield you enough to separate you from the world so you can hear and seek God's voice clearer.

I pray that you then see how all of it is connected and that it's not always people who are seeking to harm, but the Enemy and his demons who sole purpose is to destroy your testimony and silence you from sharing the Gospel.

No one who is a born again Christian was always that way, but only by the Blood of Jesus Christ are any of us made clean and whole and forgiven. Even when our past tries to pull us down, we know where those thoughts, words, energy are coming from. And that is when no weapon formed against me shall prosper makes sense. (Isaiah 54:17)

HOW COULD THIS HAPPEN TO SOMEONE LIKE ME.

Emphatically, this wouldn't have happened to me or to his family if chastity and fidelity were still honored in our culture. They don't. And they haven't been for 40 years. This. The way I had lived my life. The way that countless people live their lives for now two generations is how someone like me could easily find myself in a situation like this. Our culture is the type of culture where cheating and double lives and divorces and addictions are normal. The first sexual predator I knew was the father of my former classmate, President Bill Clinton. His sex scandal broke my senior year in high school, the year Chelsea started college at Stanford. Monica was only a couple of years older than us.

The sexual revolution has created lifetimes of living through nightmares.

It's the reason why alleged political conservatives have no problem with the fact that a current Republican nominee in Maryland is the wife of a strip club owner. Everyone places their attention to the abandoned buildings, but they forget that it is the sex industry that is the most powerful industry in the City of Baltimore, just like other cities I would imagine. And we are all expected to remain silent. *Stop being a prude. Stop projecting your guilt on others.* As a survivor, I am one of the only people who will ever speak up about any of this because we have all accepted these low expectations for everything.

In my opinion the lack of moral standards is the reason why:

- As of the date of the first publication of this book, 3,554 homicides have occurred in Baltimore since 2007[i]
- Suicide rates among children are on the rise[ii]
- There are 17,000 abandoned buildings in the City of Baltimore[iii]

- It is why 25 million people are being trafficked at this very moment around the world.[iv]
- It is why one out of four parents are unmarried.[v]
- Only half of American adults are married as compared to 72% in 1960.[vi]
- 86% of women have had premarital sex and 90% of men (age range 15-49) according to the CDC.[vii]

It feels like a lifetime ago when all this started to unravel. It is because it was.

It was 1963 when Betty Friedan wrote about "the problem that has no name" in *The Feminine Mystique*. Our generation always thought that the Women's Movement and the Sexual Revolution were the same thing. But they were never meant to be. The former wanted women to be able to express themselves creatively. Work outside the home, but initially abortion was never included as a need, want or desire of the Women's Movement. Until the Sexual Revolution raped it. People at Cosmo magazine were the ones who wanted to encourage sex without consequences. F your way to the top if you have to. Have sex free of the biological consequences.

Just like men.

Arguably the greatest hostile take over in history is all chronicled by investigative journalist Sue Ellen Browder in her 2015 book, Subverted: How I Helped The Sexual Revolution Hijack the Women's Movement. Before I heard about this book, even I thought they were one and the same this entire time. But Browder painstakingly illustrates how powerful propaganda and anti-Christian values merged the Sexual Revolution and Abortionism to the Women's Movement in order to gain the traction they needed to transform society.

> "to own and control your own body" (Abortionist Margaret Sanger)[viii]

> 'the complete legalization of abortion is the one just and inevitable answer to the question for feminine freedom" (Abortionist Larry Lader)[ix]

Browder sums the thinking up by writing, "an allegedly smart woman could biologically neuter herself (temporarily or permanently) through the Pill, the IUD, abortion, sterilization, or hysterectomy. Then viola! Suddenly, she could behave like a man both in bed and at work."[x]

Remember, you cannot change a culture concentrated on sex if you do not get women to play along.

Were there obstacles for women in the workforce then and perhaps still, yes. But until you realize that only 57 women voted to include abortion in the 1967 NOW (National Organization of Women) platform after every single woman of color and Christian walked out of the room in The Mayflower Hotel, you will not begin to appreciate how much of a farce we all have been proliferating.

Before, I was a feminist without ever thinking there was an option not to be. I haven't mentioned yet, but I was a sorority girl in college. I wasn't just a member. I was Chapter President. Greek Woman of the Year, literally. I loved what we stood for. Women's Empowerment. Sisterhood. Encouragement. Ironically enough, our philanthropy was (is) Domestic Violence. So what if we were the motley crew on campus. We weren't the rich girls or the most popular. We were just a solid sisterhood. But we were also not the greatest saints. We were party girls. Some of us more than others. As "liberated" as I was, I hadn't lost my virginity until I was 21 and that was considered old when I was in college. Fellow Greeks actually respected that about me. Since so few women at Columbia were virgins. It was like I had dozens of Big Brothers looking out for me. We all thought we were being responsible.

Even before I joined Alpha Chi Omega, sex was everywhere on campus. During first year orientation, that culture was a bit jarring for me, I admit. I was rather sheltered growing up. So, when I saw bowls of condoms laying around in the bathrooms and student activity sponsored classes on how to use dental dams, I sort of thought it was a bit much even then. And this was back in 1998. I cannot imagine how it is now. For me, I was an "adult" by the time I was exposed to any of this. Now, it is becoming rare for children to remain children anymore.

When it came to pursuing my profession, I honestly didn't think much about marriage until recently. By the time I graduated from law school at the age of 26, I almost forgot that people got married around that time. And after my main ex cheated on me had a child and still remained an alcoholic, I was already 31. Registered for business school at Maryland to rescue myself from oblivion, and by 34 ran my first political campaign. I received my first nomination to Congress by 38, and will know by the Spring if this is the end of the road politically for me now that I am 40.

No children though I've been asked that question ever since I entered into politics. Never been pregnant even though my opponents are spreading the strange rumor that I used to work for Planned Parenthood and had an abortion. Again, I've never been pregnant. Would I like to marry and be a mom still? Totally. No one really tells you that at a certain point in time the available men are either divorced already and don't want to get married again. They have had children and don't want to have anymore. Were married and got snipped and so they cannot physically have kids again. Or they are psycho like _____.

This entire time I sort of thought that personal life and political issues were separate. Just like I thought that separation of church and state was like an actual founding doctrine, which it is not in the way that it has been exploited.

It took this last Special Election to realize that all of it is connected to one thing – the destruction of our culture.

Sex was the weapon of choice. Think about it.

We are bombarded by sex and really sin everywhere. All the time. In everything. Through everything. And I did not realize the intensity until I started attending a conservative church in 2018. Honest to Pete.

ALL OF IT IS A PART OF THE BIGGER PICTURE.

Abortion was and has always been the atomic bomb to America.

Much to even my party's chagrin, the biggest political issue that I had a 180 shift on was Abortion. This may come as a surprise to Democrats, but Republicans are now forced to not talk about Abortion even when they are conservatives. Established Republicans will say, "Roe v. Wade is settled law." "It's the Law of the Land." Or "don't talk about it because it's not a *winning issue*." Every time I heard this so-called advice, I mean from some of the highest ranking members of my political party, it never sat well with me. If even Republicans can't talk about being Pro-Life, then who else would be left to represent the alternative view.

I never thought I would be a Pro-Life activist even though I was raised Catholic. This compromise or political stance is what I would later learn is called the Catholic Strategy.[xi] Even if you were a Catholic and personally Pro-Life, in public or for political purposes, you had to be Pro-Choice. I accepted this reality without ever thinking that it was a concerted plan by the Abortion Industry to get us Catholics to accept Abortion or at the very least not stand in the way of normalizing the act in our "modern" culture. Besides what would we want? To return to "back alley abortions" or even better, "we can't legislate morality!" Or "people are going to have sex anyway so the very least we should do is support birth control." Some of my fellow conservative politicos will say that they are for over-the-counter birth control since they are for prevention. And its ok since they're still against Abortions. They can't face the fact that birth control is an abortifacient – a drug that will end a pregnancy if one is developing.

To not be Pro-Choice is an anomaly for practically anyone these days, particularly for women and specifically we who are under the age of 50. I am still shocked when I hear older Black men on the campaign trail say "it's a woman's body and her right to choose." They have no idea that those exact words are elements of a marketing campaign like Nike: Just Do It. If ever we are known to believe that **Life begins at conception**, we are made to think we are weird or antiquated or forcing our religious views on society. Lest we forget the greatest fallacy of them all: Separation of Church and State.

But that is the irony of all ironies. We all are now accepting, promoting, or condoning an actual religious view that has been force fed to us – Atheism (or Humanism) within the guise of secularism underneath the purview of freedom and equality. Many of us have never really considered what these cats stood for, but if you read what they think, you will quickly realize that it is their religion that our government has grown to support, and not our shared traditional norm.

First and foremost, their slogan is "Good without God." (Visit AmericanHumanist.org if you care to wander in the poppy field). I am taking the time and attention to share this information with you because the people who promoted Abortion in the 1960s and 1970s, the folks who fought so hard to normalize "death before birth" Larry Lader and Betty Friedan were humanists.[xii] Folks probably have heard of the feminist Betty Freidan, but probably have no clue who Lawrence (Larry) Lader was. He was the guy who said that pregnancy is the "ultimate punishment of sex" in his 1973 book, *Abortion II: Making the Revolution*.[xiii] Lader was the one person whose personal mission was to legalize Abortion. His propaganda book, *Abortion*, would be used by Supreme Court Justice Harry Blackmun and his law clerk George Frampton to justify their deciding opinion for *Roe v. Wade*.[xiv] Keep in mind that Margaret Sanger was the greatest influence on Lader's life. Not Yahweh as he was originally Jewish. Sanger.[xv]

This is what the proud parents of the Abortion Industry believed:

Humanist Manifesto
Copyright © 1933 by *The New Humanist* and 1973 by the American Humanist Association[xvi]
Emphasis added.

The time has come for widespread recognition of the <u>radical changes</u> in religious beliefs throughout the <u>modern world</u>. The time is past for <u>mere revision of traditional attitudes</u>. Science and economic change have disrupted the <u>old beliefs</u>. Religions the world over are under the necessity of coming to terms with new conditions created by a <u>vastly increased knowledge and experience</u>. In every field of human activity, the vital movement is now in the direction of a candid and <u>explicit humanism</u>. In order that **religious humanism** may be better understood we, the undersigned, desire to make certain affirmations which we believe the facts of our contemporary life demonstrate.

There is great danger of a final, and we believe fatal, identification of the word religion with doctrines and methods <u>which have lost their significance</u> and <u>which are powerless to solve the problem of human living in the Twentieth Century</u>. Religions have always been means for realizing the highest values of life. Their end has been accomplished through the interpretation of the total environing situation (theology or world view), the sense of values resulting therefrom (goal or ideal), and the technique (**cult**), established for realizing the satisfactory life. A change in any of these factors results in alteration of the outward forms of religion. This fact explains the changefulness of religions through the centuries. But through all changes religion itself remains constant in its quest for abiding values, an inseparable feature of human life.

Today man's **larger understanding of the universe**, his scientific achievements, and **deeper appreciation of brotherhood**, have created a situation which **requires a new statement of the means and purposes of religion**. Such a vital, fearless, and frank religion capable of furnishing adequate social goals and personal satisfactions may appear to many people as a complete break with the past. While this age does owe a vast debt to the traditional religions, it is none the less obvious that any religion that can hope to be a synthesizing and dynamic force for today must be shaped for the needs of this age. **To establish such a religion is a major necessity of the present**. It is a responsibility **which rests upon this generation**. We therefore affirm the following:

FIRST: Religious humanists regard the universe as self-existing and not created.

SECOND: Humanism believes that man is a part of nature and that he has emerged as a result of a continuous process.

THIRD: Holding an organic view of life, humanists find that the traditional dualism of mind and body must be rejected.

FOURTH: Humanism recognizes that man's religious culture and civilization, as clearly depicted by anthropology and history, are the product of a gradual development due to his interaction with his natural environment and with his social heritage. The individual born into a particular culture is largely molded by that culture.

FIFTH: Humanism asserts that the nature of the universe depicted by modern science makes unacceptable any supernatural or cosmic guarantees of human values. Obviously humanism does not deny the possibility of realities as yet undiscovered, but it does insist that the way to determine the existence and value of any and all realities is by means of intelligent inquiry and by the assessment of their relations to human needs. Religion must formulate its hopes and plans in the light of the scientific spirit and method.

SIXTH: We are convinced that the time has passed for theism, deism, modernism, and the several varieties of "new thought".

SEVENTH: Religion consists of those actions, purposes, and experiences which are humanly significant. Nothing human is alien to the religious. It includes labor, art, science, philosophy, love, friendship, recreation—all that is in its degree expressive of intelligently satisfying human living. The distinction between the sacred and the secular can no longer be maintained.

EIGHTH: Religious Humanism considers the complete realization of human personality to be the end of man's life and seeks its development and fulfillment in the here and now. This is the explanation of the humanist's social passion.

NINTH: In the place of the old attitudes involved in worship and prayer the humanist finds his religious emotions expressed in a heightened sense of personal life and in a cooperative effort to promote social well-being.

TENTH: It follows that there will be no uniquely religious emotions and attitudes of the kind hitherto associated with belief in the supernatural.

ELEVENTH: Man will learn to face the crises of life in terms of his knowledge of their naturalness and probability. Reasonable and manly attitudes will be fostered by education and supported by custom. We assume that humanism will take the path of social and mental hygiene and discourage sentimental and unreal hopes and wishful thinking.

TWELFTH: Believing that religion must work increasingly for joy in living, religious humanists aim to foster the creative in man and to encourage achievements that add to the satisfactions of life.

THIRTEENTH: Religious humanism maintains that all associations and institutions exist for the fulfillment of human life. The intelligent evaluation, transformation, control, and direction of such associations and institutions with a view to the enhancement of human life is the purpose and program of humanism. Certainly religious institutions, their ritualistic forms, ecclesiastical methods, and communal activities must be reconstituted as rapidly as experience allows, in order to function effectively in the modern world.

FOURTEENTH: <u>The humanists are firmly convinced that existing acquisitive and profit-motivated society has shown itself to be inadequate and that a radical change in methods, controls, and motives must be instituted. A socialized and cooperative economic order must be established to the end that the equitable distribution of the means of life be possible. The goal of humanism is a free and universal society in which people voluntarily and intelligently cooperate for the common good. Humanists demand a shared life in a shared world.</u>

FIFTEENTH AND LAST: We assert that humanism will: (a) affirm life rather than deny it; (b) seek to elicit the possibilities of life, not flee from them; and (c) endeavor to establish the conditions of a satisfactory life for all, not merely for the few. By this positive morale and intention humanism will be guided, and from this perspective and alignment the techniques and efforts of humanism will flow.

So stand the theses of religious humanism. Though we consider the religious forms and **ideas of our fathers no longer adequate**, the quest for the good life is still the central task for mankind. **Man** is at last **becoming**

aware that he alone is responsible for the realization of the world of his dreams, that he has within himself the power for its achievement. He must set intelligence and will to the task.

If you read through any or all of the above "Humanist Manifesto" you will quickly see that it is not only a religion, but it seeks to replace largely held beliefs with what they consider is right. Not Truth. Their truth. Because it is their opinion that everything else is old fashioned and inadequate to address "modern" life – and let's not forget this is 1973. Humanist believe that the God of Abraham, Isaac, and Jesus was obsolete even back then.

Folks who believe in "Humanism" used to be fringe and counter-culture, but more than 40 years or four (4) decades – MY LIFETIME – this worldview or religion has taken over our culture to a point where virtually everything and everyone is controlled by it. Not Jesus Christ. Not God. Not the Holy Spirit. It. The "Humanists" of the 1970s were the intellectual powerhouses that influenced the young people of their day like future presidential frontrunner Bernie Sanders (who was 31/32 years old), Senator Elizabeth Warren (24 years old in 1973), and Hillary Clinton (26 at the time). These future leaders of the Democrat Party are just a sprinkling of the most powerful "Humanists" that use their religion to promote their closely held beliefs through and onto American society. I personally have no idea who in the Republican Party espouses this religious belief, but I will not be surprised when I meet them. More than likely they will be moderates who think that people like me are extremists for believing in the power of Jesus Christ and supremacy of God.

If you are being honest, every one of their beliefs is Anti-Christ (opposed to, against, destroying or disabling, situated opposite)[xvii]:

1) Old religions are powerless and useless.
2) They believe that the universe was not created.
3) The concept of Mind and Body are rejected.
4) They restrict religion to time and location.
5) They believe that the universe revolves around humans and their needs only.
6) Sacred and secular are not distinct.
7) A human dies and there is nothing after death.
8) Traditional religion is sentimental, unrealistic and wishful thinking.

9) Churches have to change in order to modernize.
10) They believe socialism is the only form of economy that will work.

This may be the first time you have ever heard of the word or the religion of Humanism, but it is not the first time you have encountered the belief structure. The Green New Deal. Universal Healthcare. Separation of Church and State. Secularism in Public School. Devaluing of God-centered Schools. Downplaying of Traditional Religions. Insistence that the Founders of America were either bigots or religious fanatics or their ancestors, deists. And last but certainly not least, Abortion are all tools that humanists have used over the last four and half decades to insert their beliefs on and throughout our culture. Just think about it. If you can get a woman to kill their baby, you can get them to accept anything. The only way you can get a woman to kill her baby is to get her to forget God, and her connection to Him through Christ.

"For thou hast possessed my reins: thou hast covered me in my mother's womb.

I will praise thee: for I am fearfully and wonderfully made: marvelous are thy works: and that my soul knoweth right well."

Psalm 139:13-14

Move along. Nothing to see here.

If you ask me, I don't think a true Christian can be elected to Congress these days, at least not for the first time and not from the East Coast or California. I have personally witnessed the degradation of the Democrat Party and have had to accept that the Republican Party has acquiesced so much to secularism, it too is very close to falling off the cliff beyond the point of no return.

Beyond the "powers that be", however, the greatest threat to our republic and our God-led nation, is the impact that all this has on the "average" citizen. So many people are purposefully left in the dark or silenced/mocked to speak the truth. Without a literal **Come to Jesus** moment very, very, very, very, very soon, all bets are off.

NOW DO YOU SEE?

If you don't see what I mean by now, I get it. I sound like an old fuddy-duddy, hyper religious, right-wing, ultra-conservative woman who is out of touch. The thing is, I am not. I've been so involved in this world that I had no idea until I stepped out of it. And yes, broke the spell. It is also a matter of generations.

I'm technically a part of the baby-boomer generation but am a Gen-X/Older Millennial. My wonderful father, may he rest in God's Eternal Peace, William Earle Matory, Sr, was born in 1928. So my rearing was already more conservative than my peers at Sidwell and Columbia. My upbringing is probably the main reason why my life wasn't more messed up than it ended up. Plus mom being originally from the Philippines, my home training was Christian. It was the scholastic and outward environment that was infused with this humanist, moral relativism mindset. But at every step, I benefitted from having a conservative lens to run ideas through. Clearly, I did not follow the path that I was told to follow, but I always had a moral compass to consider. At the very least. I can state that plainly.

The very concepts of family, husband, father, wife, mother, even child have been so disfigured by humanism/abortionism/socialism (it's all the same thing), that we all have seemed to have forgotten how important the American Family was to our founding. This culture forces us to believe that all the founders were old, white bigoted, misogynists and that anything they did must be destroyed solely because they did it. The very idea is unsustainable if you actually want this country to succeed. That's the point – These cats don't want us to succeed.

The American Family was at the heart of the birth, growth, and sustainability of our country. People place so much attention on the economy, but they forget that the family is the first unit of governance and closest compact in economics there will ever be.

There is certainly no country in the world where the tie of
marriage is more respected than in America, or where conjugal
happiness is more highly or worthily appreciated. In Europe
almost all the disturbances of society arise from the
irregularities of domestic life. (De Tocqueville, Democracy in
America)

Men and women were considered equal under the laws of God.

The roles of husbands and wives were considered equally   important.

All biblical roots as described in the book, The 5,000 Year Leap: A Miracle that Changed the World by W. Cleon Skousen (1981).[xviii]

We have forgotten that the co-founder of NOW for example, Ms. Kate Millett, was a cultural Marxist, and that the proud consciously aware, hyper-empowered feminist believed that the Cultural Revolution would be brought about by "destroying the American family." "Patriarchy was thought to be the worst form of evil and by destroying that (the role of fathers and husbands) they could successfully destroy the family.[xix] They would do so by promoting promiscuity and infidelity.[xx] Again, everyone wants to focus on women and their role/choice/decision/act of Abortion, but they forget that it was equally an effective tool to erase the responsibility of men and allow them to dive fully into sin with "no repercussions." Again, remember strip clubs are just as normalized as mass murder and inter-generational poverty.

Move along. Nothing to see here.

Like many former liberals turned conservatives/Christians, there was a breaking point for me when it came to the overreaching nature of the socialist/humanist/anti-christ(ian) values that have seeped into our culture. For me, and many other Black Americans, it was legitimizing same-sex marriage, coupled with the transgender agenda. Again, this is where it gets out of hand. I have had gay and lesbian friends since I was 13/14 years old and actually some of my lesbian friends are now transgender men. Irony of ironies who are more successful professionally as trans-men than they would have been as regular lesbian women. They were also the first gay marriages that I knew about. I supported them individually and appreciated the discrimination etc. But what we are witnessing now is something totally different than in the 1990s/2000s.

I never witnessed two virgins marry each other until 2019 when I attended the wedding of my pastor's daughter.

Now, anyone who is honest, will notice the hyper-sexualization and hyper-promiscuity nature of everything. Things have gotten so out of hand that folks are pushing for pedophilia. Children selling themselves directly to the highest bidder on-line. Selling their little brothers and sisters to be sexually mutilated. How in the world is this our new normal, if it wasn't by design.

Conservatives have spent all their time and attention to the economic aspect of socialism. They missed the cultural component all together. And perhaps it may be too late.

Here is my understanding of the stages of cultural deterioration/socialism. This is how I have observed it in my life:

Step 1: Encourage pre-marital sex and make it a norm. Let folks be comfortable with casual sin, I mean sex.

Step 2: Allow for no-fault divorce. Marriage is no longer God-centered.

Step 3: Make sex and provocative attire seem common place. So women will forget that they are still being seen
as sex objects.

Step 4: Promote machismo culture for boys and young men. So they forget what chivalry and respect actually look like.

Step 5: Take over the schools and media so no one can really see what you're doing to a culture because you control everything.

Step 6: Place doubt around traditional religion, specifically Christianity.

Step 7: Take over the political system.

Step 8: Make Abortion seem more like a haircut than murder.

Step 9: Use murder and mayhem as a distraction if more people figure things out.

As I have spent more time in politics, I realize how many people have no idea what Socialism/Communism actually is. I did not really until I found myself wondering what all was going on and why there were so many elected officials in Maryland who were unapologetically socialists. It is actually more acceptable to be a socialist in the State of Maryland than it is to be a conservative or a Christian. It is heartbreaking to know that the Black Churches are at the heart of a lot of the misinformation.

The Manifesto of the Communist Party was first published in 1848, before the American Civil War. The theories and beliefs surrounding the "proletariat" (the working man) and the "bourgeoisie" (the ruling class) were cooked and considered before the economic strides of Reconstruction or the Industrial Revolution. Its first fundamental flaw, especially in an American context, is that these two "distinctions" were permanent or generational. Putting aside the scribes were both bourgie to begin with, they never considered or would have considered a society that economic agility and generational strides could be made (or lost).

Do Americans ever consider what measures are

proscribed to engineer the Communist Utopia?

1)   Abolition of property

2)   Heavy taxes

3)   Abolition of all inheritance

4)   Confiscation of the property of all emigrants and rebels.

5)   Centralisation of credit in the hands of the State, by means of a
national bank with State capital and an exclusive monopoly

6)   Centralisation of the means of communication and transport in
the hands of the State.[xxi]

That is just the first six stated in the infamous Manifesto. The Principles of Communism are even more overt.

For example:

21. What will be the influence of communist society on the family?

It will transform the relations between the sexes into a purely private matter which concerns only the persons involved and into which society has no   occasion to intervene. It can do this since it does away with private property and   *educates children on a communal basis*, and in this way removes the two   bases of *traditional marriage* – the dependence rooted in private property, of   the woman on the man, and of the children on the parents.

And here is the answer to the outcry of the highly moral philistines against the "community of women". Community of women is a condition which belongs   entirely to bourgeois society and which today finds its complete expression in   prostitution. But prostitution is based on private property and falls with it. Thus, communist society, instead of introducing community of women, in fact abolishes   it.

22. What will be the attitude of communism to existing nationalities?

The nationalities of the peoples associating themselves in accordance   with the principles of community *will be compelled to mingle with each other*   as a result of this association and thereby *to dissolve themselves*, just as the   various estate and class distinctions must disappear through abolition of their   basis, private property.

23. What will be its attitude to existing religions?

All religions so far have been the expression of historical stages of   development of individual peoples or groups of peoples. But *communism is the   stage of historical development which makes all existing religions   superfluous and brings about their disappearance.*

24. How do communists differ from socialists?

"The so-called socialists are divided into three categories:

1. Reactionary Socialists

2. Bourgeois Socialists

3. **DEMOCRATIC SOCIALISTS** (emphasis added)[xxii]

Now do you see how all of these "revolutions" lead us to this point in history and culture?

The only thing that can stop the socialist takeover of our society is the return to believing in the One True God and accepting the Messiah as the Messiah. Go directly to The Source.

None of the aforementioned "fallenness" would have happened so easily if we all had not stepped away from traditional values.

It's that simple because it was that deliberate. No point in searching for other manmade solutions when the religious component is what was destroyed in the first place. Fix that and you will fix everything else. If you do not see the connections by now, you have allowed the Enemy to take over your thoughts.

NOW IS THE TIME.

If you really want to get off the roller coaster and start to know your real place in time and space, then accept the gift of salvation. You have probably heard of Heaven and Hell. But you probably didn't realize that there is no such thing as Purgatory. Everyone is going to Hell for eternity. Unless and until you accept the Messiah as your Personal Lord and Savior, no acts or rosaries are getting you to Heaven. Just appreciate God through Christ, and accept your proper inheritance.

This is the only thing that will exclaim our world. Any other explanation falls short.

Here is the Romans Road.*

* The Book of Romans was written by the Apostle Paul who before becoming a follower of Christ persecuted Christians for a living. His name was Saul then. So when people refer to extreme transformations of the heart, Saul to Paul is the perfect example of the power of the Holy Spirit working through someone's life.

First Stop: "For all have sinned, and come short of the glory of God." Romans 3:23

Second Stop: "For the wages of sin is death; but the gift of God is eternal life through Jesus Christ our Lord." Romans 6:23

Third Stop: "But God commendeth his love towards us, in that, while we were yet sinners, Christ died for us." Romans 5:8

Fourth Stop: "That if thou shalt confess with thy mouth the Lord Jesus, and shalt believe in thine heart that God hath raised him from the dead, thou shalt be saved.

  For with the heart man believeth unto righteousness; and with the mouth confession is made unto salvation." Romans 10:9-10

Fifth Stop: "For whosoever shall call upon the name of the Lord shall be saved." Romans 10:13

It is that simple. But it is not easy.

It is a conscious, deliberate acceptance of Christ as the Messiah. You must believe that He alone forgives us our sins and brings us to everlasting life. Not a priest, not a pope, no man or woman. Only Jesus.

You also have to accept the fact that there is sin and that it is bad. This simple fact runs counter to the culture of the now. Do you see why we have been made to think the way we do now? Again, there is a purpose for all of it, but you have the power to change everything.

PART TWO
21-DAY DEVOTIONAL

I would love to share with you a gift.

Getting saved from Hell is amazing, but another cool thing about becoming a Christian is that you become a part of this new Christian family. It really does not matter where you are from or what got you to accept Jesus as your personal Lord and Savior, but what matters is that you will never ever be alone. You now and forever will be a sister or brother in Christ. There is a world of people out here that will help you along your journey. You can reach out to them, but nothing and no one will compare to reading directly from the Bible and hearing directly from God Himself.

So, this 21-Day Devotional includes the favorite

bible verses from some of my new Christian family. Some folks are fellow congregation members, and others are Christians who have witnessed to me on Facebook.

Why 21 days? It is said that it takes about twenty-one days to break and make a new habit. This journey through our new life is going to take the rest of our lives, but start somewhere. Start here. Start now.

We pray that these are a blessing to you. Whenever you feel yourself stumbling, go right back to the Lord and He will be your true comfort.

†

Please note all verses will come from the King James Version of the Bible. If you have access to a concordance (on-line, a reference guide that helps refer to the Greek and Hebrew translations), you will get a greater understanding about what the Lord is saying to you.

May God continue to Bless You and may the Holy Spirit guide your thoughts, words, feelings, and steps.

DAY ONE

Serve the LORD with gladness: come before his presence with singing.

Psalm 100:2

Submitted by Pastor Shiflett, Dundalk, MD

How are you approaching the Lord? Where? When? If you think about it, we are in the presence of the Lord all the time and we serve him through everything we do. See today. Are you working with gladness? With joy? No matter what your signing voice is, God doesn't care how well you sing. Have joy. Find joy in whatever you do today.

NOTES

DAY TWO

For ye are bought with a price: therefore glorify God in your body, and in your spirit, which are God's.

1 Cor 6:20

Submitted by Christopher R., Dundalk, MD

If ever you forget, Jesus not only died on the cross for our salvation, He came down knowing that it would end that way and he did it anyway. Your eternal life was bought when Christ became mortal. He didn't have to, but he did. We now get to praise Him with our spirit and don't forget your body as well. Today, hold your head high and let your spirit shine knowing that God gave his life, so you can redeem yours. Ask yourself: Does It Glorify God?

NOTES

DAY THREE

The LORD is my portion, saith my soul; therefore will I hope in him. The LORD is good unto them that wait for him, to the soul that seeketh him.

Lamentations 3:24, 25

Submitted by Grace S, Dundalk, MD

I will admit waiting on the Lord is still one of my greatest challenges as a new Christian. Especially whether to take an action or remain silent. Especially in this culture, we want everything now. We cannot stand waiting. But isn't it wonderful to know that God is everything for us. He will provide, especially when we wait on Him and seek him first. Today, remember. For every need, hope and wait on God.

NOTES

DAY FOUR

Let the words of my mouth, and the meditation of my heart, be acceptable in thy sight, O LORD, my strength, and my redeemer.

Psalm 19:14

Submitted by Hannah K., Meriden, CT

I love this verse. So much humility. We ought to ask whether our words and attention and intentions are in line with God. This is a good way to keep check of your words, thoughts and feelings. Run them by Him first.

NOTES

DAY FIVE

Fear thou not; for I am with thee: be not dismayed; for I am thy God: I will strengthen thee; yea, I will help thee; yea, I will uphold thee with the right hand of my righteousness.

Isaiah 41:10

Submitted by Laurel S., Boca Raton, FL

This one is when you need to dig deep. Fear thou not! God is with you. Don't worry. God is your god. He will give you strength. When you know you don't have anything left in you. How great is that. You have God! In all matters. You have Him. And He has you.

NOTES

DAY SIX

For God sent not his Son into the world to condemn the world; but that the world through him might be saved.

John 3:17

Submitted by Winnie H., St. Louis, MO

Especially nowadays. It seems like people think that Christianity and Jesus is a major burden or problem. Just the opposite. The Messiah became man, lived a full life, and was crucified to save the world from damnation. God sent his son to save us all from an eternity of destruction. Today, find peace and comfort in knowing that Jesus saved you when you accepted the gift of redemption. Smile. Rejoice. And share the good news.

NOTES

DAY SEVEN

And whatsoever ye do, do it heartily, as to the Lord, and not unto men.

Colossians 3:23

Submitted by Michael B., Atlanta, GA

Another good one for this day and age. Our culture forces us to care so much about what other people think of us, we should only be seeking the approval of God, not man. Catch yourself today. Whatever you're doing, do it fully with all your heart for Him and not them.

NOTES

DAY EIGHT

The Lord is my shepherd; I shall not want.

Psalm 23:1

Submitted by James N., Dundalk, MD

You might as well read the entire Psalm 23. It is probably the best six sentences ever written in the history of written word. I mean. It gets it in. Highs and lows. The LORD is with you. Always remember this. You cannot, need not, ought not want anything else besides the Lord. Everything and everyone with fall short. He is responsible for your life as he is your shepherd. He will provide. He will protect. Do not fear. God's got you.

NOTES

DAY NINE

And when the woman saw that the tree was good for food, and that it was pleasant to the eyes, and a tree to be desired to make one wise, she took of the fruit thereof, and did eat, and gave also unto her husband with her, and he did eat.

Exodus 3:6

Submitted by Marcel L., from Facebook

This is where it all started to go downhill from here. God told them distinctly stay away, and what did they do, they went and did it anyway. From then on, man fell. So remember that whenever you're dealing with anyone who may have forgotten how to act or speak. Maybe that person is you. It happens. We are all sinners who fall short. Be mindful and forgive. Ask for forgiveness. And honor God..

NOTES

DAY TEN

Jesus said unto her, I am the resurrection, and the life: he that believeth in me, though he were dead, yet shall he live: and whosoever liveth and believeth in me shall never die. Believest thou this?

John 11: 25-26

Submitted by Erin J., From Facebook

Arguably the greatest miracles that Jesus ever performed on another person is the resurrection of Lazarus. Martha comes up to Jesus angry that he let her brother Lazarus die. The reality is he died, but the truth is Martha doubted Jesus. How many times did we doubt Jesus's ability because of what we thought he did not do? This is the power in believing in and trusting on Jesus. Straight up miracles happen. He can and has raised the dead to live again. He has already done that for you when you accepted Him as your lord and savior. Can you trust in Him to do other miracles for you too?

NOTES

DAY ELEVEN

Teaching them to observe all things whatsoever I have commanded you: and, lo, I am with you always, even unto the end of the world. Amen.

Matthew 28:20

Submitted by April I., Havre de Grace, MD

This is the last verse of the Great Commission when Jesus tells his disciples to spread the Gospel or "the Good News". What blessed assurance it is to know that Jesus is with you always, like all the time for all time. He is with you all the way until the end of the world. Do you feel like God doesn't see you? Like you're doing everything you think you can to honor Him, but nothing is changing. That is of course your point of view. It may be easier said than done, but don't worry. He said he would be with us always. Even though you may not see, Jesus is there. Have faith (and patience).

NOTES

DAY TWELVE

Ye are of God, little children, and have overcome them: because greater is he that is in you, than he that is in the world.

I John 4:4

Submitted by Kristi S., Dundalk, MD

So you are awesome. Like really. Amazing. Have you forgotten whose you are? You are of God. And whatever obstacles or challenges or enemies or strongholds that you face, you have overcome them already simply because God is within you. Nothing in this world is greater than Him. Did you forget already? Is there a situation that triggers your doubt? Whatever and whenever that is just remember: You are a child of the one true God. You are the sibling of Jesus. The greatest Father. The best brother ever. You are theirs.

NOTES

DAY THIRTEEN

For I know him, that he will command his children and his household after him, and they shall keep the way of the LORD, to do justice and judgment; that the LORD may bring upon Abraham that which he hath spoken of him.

Genesis 18:19

Submitted by Edward K., Englewood, CO

Is there a situation or a person that you think you have to reach out to, but it brings you to a place that you don't desire to go? In Abraham's case, that was Sodom. Yikes. Do you think that person or situation once you connect with them will do the right thing and follow God? Are you sure? Make sure you stay close to God. Do not be tempted. Stay focused. God will answer your prayers.

NOTES

DAY FOURTEEN

And I heard a great voice out of heaven saying, Behold, the tabernacle of God is with men, and he will dwell with them, and they shall be his people, and God himself shall be with them, and be their God.

And God shall wipe away all tears from their eyes; and there shall be no more death, neither sorrow, nor crying, neither shall there be any more pain: for the former things are passed away.

And he that sat upon the throne said, Behold, I make all things new. And he said unto me, Write: for these words are true and faithful.

Revelation 21:3-5

Submitted by Ramona W., Alexandria, VA

Usually, the Book of Revelation sounds like something scary, but remember, since you picked the right side in the battle, it is actually something to look forward to for followers of Christ. No more tears. No more pain. No more crying. No more death even. He makes all things new. Can you keep this in mind as you go through today? This powerful glory erases every single problem you have, are, or will face. Alleluia.

NOTES

DAY FIFTEEN

From the end of the earth will I cry unto thee, when my heart is overwhelmed: lead me to the rock that is higher than I.

Psalm 61:2

Submitted by Grace R., Dundalk, MD

It's totally ok to cry. Cry out to God, especially when you are at your wits end. Can you ask God to bring you to a better place, a better situation? Of course you can. That's what He is really good at. (I know that sentence ended in a preposition). But focus. On God. Let Him know. He wants to hear from you, and wipe your tears away. Remember, you are His child, and He will take care of you. Continue to believe.

NOTES

DAY SIXTEEN

*Every good gift and every perfect gift is from above, and
cometh down from the Father of lights, with whom is no
variableness, neither shadow of turning.*

James 1:17

Submitted by Carol F., Ocean Pines, MD

God's gifts are blessings never curses. They are
never shady or sketchy. Is there something or
maybe someone in your life that causes you
uncertainty or high anxiety? Are you sure it is a
blessing from God? You may need to spend a
little more time in your prayer closet on that one.
Listen closely, quietly for God's word. His gifts
are perfect and good.

NOTES

DAY SEVENTEEN

A soft answer turneth away wrath: but grievous words stir up anger.

Proverbs 15:1

Submitted by Juan J., Philadelphia, PA

Words are powerful. So is the energy that you place within them. In this age of texting and social media, and the cultural climate to boot, everyone seems to be on edge. We must be more mindful about how we express ourselves. As followers of Christ, there is a higher expectation. I know I still have an issue with this myself. But as you go through the day, wait before you answer. Find a easier way of responding, particularly when you are trying to keep the peace. This one may take more practice. Be kind to yourself.

NOTES

DAY EIGHTEEN

Now unto him that is able to do exceedingly abundantly above all that we ask or think, according to the power that worketh in us,

Unto him be glory in the church by Christ Jesus throughout all ages, world without end. Amen.

Ephesians 3:20-21

Submitted by Angela M., Frederick, MD

Did you forget that you serve the God of Miracles? He has the ability to do greater things than we can even imagine or request. And when those things occur, He gets the glory, rightfully so. Ask and think away for the goodness, and when God outperforms again and again, Glory Be.

NOTES

DAY NINETEEN

These things I have spoken unto you, that in me ye might have peace. In the world ye shall have tribulation: but be of good cheer; I have overcome the world.

John 16:33

Submitted by Tina S., Essex, MD

When you're saved, it doesn't mean you'll never have problems. I don't know what made us think that (I admit, I thought things would just be smooth sailing.) We are still going to have problems. But there is a distinct difference between you before and you after; now you have Jesus and he conquered everything. He will give you peace and victory. You are on the winning team.

NOTES

DAY TWENTY

Behold, I give unto you power to tread on serpents and
scorpions, and over all the power of the enemy: and nothing
shall by any means hurt you.

Luke 10:19

Submitted by Jacqueline T., Chantilly, VA

Powerful stuff, right? We sometimes forget that
God has given us power to conquer the enemy.
It is His power that works through us and
protects us. We are not alone in any battle. We
have God. The enemy will try to make you think
you are weak and helpless and alone. The first
weapon we have against the enemy is to tell him
no. Remove the negative thought out of your
head. Just uttering the name of Jesus is
kryptonite to the enemy. Try it today.

NOTES

DAY TWENTY-ONE

Let us hear the conclusion of the whole matter: Fear God, and keep his commandments: for this is the whole duty of man.

Eccl 12:13

Submitted by Caleb K., Dundalk, MD

What a good one to end on. I had no idea this was going to be the last one for the last day. Fear God. Keep his commandments. This is the only thing we are responsible for doing. Mind you this is a lifetime commitment. Are there some commandments that you have fallen short on? We all have. No one is perfect. But the point is to keep on. Repent when you mess up and keep on.

You got this!

NOTES

[Bonus Essay]

Still A Matter of Life and Death: Conservatives, Candidates Ought to Be Proudly Pro-Life by Liz Matory

Did you know that political candidates are told not to mention that they are Pro-Life? Even if they are pro-life, Catholic, Christian, Jewish, non-denominational believers in the God of Abraham and Jesus, we are told by many established members of both major parties that we can have these views in our personal lives, but "Roe v. Wade is settled law. Abortion is not a winning issue, so do not make it part of your platform." This advice is **still** given to this day, even in the era of after-birth abortions. And you wonder why our representatives do not seem to represent our actual values anymore.

I am a relatively new member of the Pro-Life movement, but even I know that Abortion is still the #1 political issue. I should say "protecting" abortion is more important than anything else. Not The Green New Deal. Not Poor People. Protecting the *Myth of Abortion* is only way to keep the American electorate hostage and divorced from science, reality, and/or God. Abortion has purposefully been preserved as a controversial issue so voters do not consider what they know is physically, spiritually, emotionally, and actually real. Even grown men have accepted the agenda's rhetoric, "a woman should have her rights" even though we all know girlfriend did not get pregnant on her own. If ever conservative candidates do state and stand as pro-life candidates, I mean *Life begins at Conception* candidates, they are either shunned or silenced because moderates do not want to lose their political capital on the one issue that they will certainly lose votes. That's what matters. Not Life. Not death. Just votes.

It's said if you want to know who is in control of politics, see what issue gets the most pushback, and that is the power that reigns supreme.

In my state of Maryland, the former Catholic colony, radical elected officials have been pushing to preserve Abortion as a constitutional right. They want women in Maryland to have a constitutional right to end the life of the other human being that grows within their womb. This state is also one of the four states that does not allow for abortions to be statistically monitored even for public health data. What is said about New York's black babies could be said about The

City of Baltimore's, if only they were thought important enough to be counted.

I never considered not being pro-choice.

After all, that's what modern, professional educated women are supposed to be. We're supposed to be *for a Woman's Right to Choose…No man ought to be able to tell us what we can and cannot do with our bodies…We shouldn't have to be relegated to back alley abortions…besides Roe v. Wade is settled law.*

Even as a raised Catholic, democrat, I thought it was still okay to be personally pro-life, but be pro-choice politically. That was until I started asking questions. Like, if I do not support late-term abortion, what advice to you have for me, NARAL representative? **Silence**.

But it's a baby. Nope. To them it's just a "lump of cells."

I will never forget in 2015 when I was an independent, a top political advisor told me that if I said I was pro-choice that she could get me lots of donor money. It was then when I knew where the money and power was really held. Not by the parties, but by the Abortion industry.

Folks always ask what was it that made me switch

or how did I get to be so conservative now. That is a long story, and it was even before I accepted Jesus as my personal Lord and Savior on November 30, 2018. But to put it simply, I allowed my mind to be open to the truth.

If we all know from 7th Grade Biology that once a sperm enters into an egg, the egg is then fertilized, and the combination of that one specific sperm and that one specific egg make one new unique human being, gender is determined even from that early point, and that the new creation develops rapidly, purposefully through every moment of 40 weeks of gestation with a woman's womb, then there is no point during that pregnancy that that unique human being stops being a human being. If all of that is real, then the "choice" of abortion is not real. That "choice" is what is actually fabricated.

And, so is the "prevention" myth of hormonal birth control, but even that is truth people are not willing to face.

The longer people continue to shy away from the truth, the more human beings will be discontinued. But who else will speak up about it, if we do not use our platforms to bring awareness and our votes to protect what is real. **Simple,**

mindful awareness will turn the tide. That is what happened to me, and that is why we must speak up about it. Darkness abhors light, but light shines brightest in the face of darkness.

The only people who can change the course of history are conservatives and conservative candidates.

Will we speak truth to power for the most powerless?

#LifeLeads - Terry Beatley, Pro-Life advocate

Ask, and it shall be given you; seek, and ye shall find; knock, and it shall be opened unto you.

Matthew 7:7

Submitted by Rita R-M. (My Mom)

Washington, DC

i Homicide rate in Baltimore, as seen on 3/6/2020
https://homicides.news.baltimoresun.com/?range=all.
ii https://www.pbs.org/newshour/health/youth-suicide-rates-are-on-the-rise-in-the-u-s as of 3/7/2020.
iii https://www.baltimoresun.com/politics/bs-md-ci-vacant-demolition-20190214-story.html as of 3/6/2020.
iv https://polarisproject.org/ as of 3/6/2020.
v https://www.pewsocialtrends.org/2018/04/25/the-changing-profile-of-unmarried-parents/ as of 3/6/2020.
vi https://www.pewsocialtrends.org/2018/04/25/the-changing-profile-of-unmarried-parents/ as of 3/6/2020.
vii https://www.cdc.gov/nchs/nsfg/key_statistics/p_2015-2017.htm#premarital as of 3/6/2020.
viii Browder, Sue Ellen, *Subverted: How I Helped the Sexual Revolution Hijack the Women's Movement* (San Francisco, Ignatius Press, 2015), 54.
ix Id., 55.
x Id., 60.
xi Beatley, Terry, What if We've Been Wrong: Keeping my promise to America's "Abortion King" (Guiding Light Books), 134.
xii Browder, 48-49.
xiii Browder, 49.
xiv Browder, 94-95.
xv Browder, 48.
xvi Humanist Manifesto as viewed on 3/4/2020 see

https://americanhumanist.org/what-is-humanism/manifesto1/.

[xvii] Definition of anti- see https://www.thefreedictionary.com/anti, as seen on 3/4/2020.

[xviii] Skousen, W.Cleon, *The 5,000 Year Leap: A Miracle that Changed the World*, (Malta, National Center for Constitutional Studies, 1981, 2013), 281-283.

[xix] Millett, Mallory, *Fact Check: Marxist, Feminism's Ruined Lives*, Hosea Initiatives.

[xx] Id.

[xxi] Marx, Karl and Frederick Engels, Manifesto of the Communist Party (1848).

[xxii] Engels, Frederick, The Principles of Communism (1847).